This Book Belongs to

SCAN TO VISIT MY AUTHOR PAGE

Join our Ministry group on facebook

https://www.facebook.com/groups/myholytrinity.co

Check out our merch at

https://fashionsbyfelicia.myecomshop.com

This book is dedicated to my Dad who taught me to be an independent and

determined person, without whom I would never be able to achieve

my dreams

ABOUT THE AUTHOR

Hello, God's children my name is Felicia Patterson, I hold a degree in psychology, aromatherapy as well as am an Ordained Minister. Journaling has helped me through some very tough times in my life along with my faith and I thought why not combine the two. I could go on about my accomplishments but instead, I would like to share with you a personal story of what the power of faith and prayer can do.

ABOUT THE AUTHOR

I was born with a rare spinal condition. My parents reached out to all the greats, but all said there was no treatment and just keep me comfortable until my time came. After months of searching and praying, a young and brilliant neurosurgeon came up with a plan that would hopefully work. Prior to what was to be a series of surgeries, I wanted to see the Happy Hunters that were a few hours away from us. Things were tight but my parents made it happen but only had fifty dollars to travel on. We got to the motel got cleaned up and walked across the street where they were giving the sermon. At this time, I had lost all function of my lower extremities and I had to be carried into the church. Prior to the sermon, they were passing the plate. We only had enough to get back home, so we don't have anything to spare. As they were passing the plate my mom put the fifty dollars in. The lady minister whom I will never forget asked my dad to sit me beside her. While her husband was giving the sermon, she was rubbing my back. My parents had communicated with them through email, but she had no knowledge of who we were or my condition. After a while, she asked my mom and another woman to take my hands and walk me around the church. I had not walked in months yet practically ran around the church. After it was over, we were headed for the lobby when the same woman that walked with me around the church came up to my mom and said, "God told me to give you this" and gave her two twenties and a ten. Our Life is a testament that through all the challenges, loss, and despair that we must hold to our faith and trust that we are all here for a purpose.

Table of Contents

Table of Contents

About your journal

Coloring Scripture

Journal

Reflect

Prayers

THE NEXT FEW PAGES WILL EXPLAIN HOW TO

USE YOUR JOURNAL

PSALMS 102

Hear my prayer, Lord;
let my cry for help come to you.
Do not hide your face from me
when I am in distress.
Turn your ear to me;
when I call, answer me quickly.
For my days vanish like smoke;
my bones burn like glowing embers.
My heart is blighted and withered like grass;
I forget to eat my food.
In my distress I groan aloud
and am reduced to skin and bones.
I am like a desert owl,
like an owl among the ruins.
I lie awake; I have become
like a bird alone on a roof.
All day long my enemies taunt me;
those who rail against me use my name as a curse.
For I eat ashes as my food
and mingle my drink with tears
because of your great wrath,
for you have taken me up and thrown me aside.
My days are like the evening shadow;
I wither away like grass.
But you, Lord, sit enthroned forever;
your renown endures through all generations.
You will arise and have compassion on Zion,
for it is time to show favor to her;
the appointed time has come.
For her stones are dear to your servants;
her very dust moves them to pity.
The nations will fear the name of the Lord,
all the kings of the earth will revere your glory.
For the Lordwill rebuild Zion
and appear in his glory.
He will respond to the prayer of the destitute;
he will not despise their plea.
Let this be written for a future generation,
that a people not yet created may praise the Lord:

Coloring Scripture

Each 52-week total features a new coloring scripture page to reflect your thoughts on throughout the week giving you time to memorize the verse and understand its true meaning. Coloring works other areas of the brain, allowing the brain a chance to relax, and the space needed to shift gears. In turn, it allows the brain time to focus on the topic at hand.

Journal

What week is it? Record the date and watch how your journey with Gods grows through the year.

What areas of your life you want to grow? Ask god to teach me.

Let God know how grateful you are. What are you thankful for this week?

What are some areas you need God's guidance? Ask for him to guide you.

Reflect

Each week also contains a "Reflect" page with questions and thoughts inspired by the weekly Scripture, as well as room to write down your thoughts. You can use this as a weekly reflection or just fill in the blanks in a single day! Remember that this journal can be customized to fit your spiritual journey.

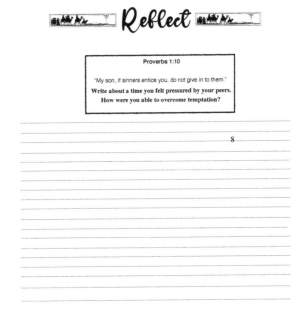

Memories, Prayers and Guidance

It's our job to guide the next generation. What do you want the future generation to know?

Record your weekly prayers.

Life is a beautiful and challenging journey. Take time to write about the

Prayers

The back of the book includes a place to

record your prayers.

Now that you know how to use your journal, trust

that the Lord will guide you with the year ahead.

EPHESIANS 4:26-27

"Be ye angry, and sin not: let not the sun go down upon your wrath: Neither give place to the devil".

15

 # Reflect

> " What does it mean to you to be a person of faith? How important is this to you?

_____
_____
_____
_____
_____
_____
_____
_____
_____
_____
_____
_____
_____
_____
_____
_____
_____
_____
_____
_____
_____

Thank You Lord

 Teach Me

 Guide Me

Future Generations

Highlight

My Prayer"s

PROVERBS 14:29

He that is slow to wrath
is of great
understanding:
but he that is hasty of
spirit exalteth folly"

19

 # Reflect

> **What's your favorite Bible story about faith?**
> **Why?**

_____
_____
_____
_____
_____
_____
_____
_____
_____
_____
_____
_____
_____
_____
_____
_____
_____
_____

Thank You Lord

Teach Me

Guide Me

Future Generations

Highlight

My Prayer"s

EXODUS 23:25

"ye shall serve the
Lord your God, and he
shall bless thy bread,
and thy water; and I
will take sickness away
from the midst of
thee".

23

 # Reflect

Colossians 4:6

"Let your conversation be always full of grace, seasoned with salt, so that you may know how to answer everyone."

How do you respond to someone who asks you about your faith? How do you share the Word of God?

Thank You Lord

♥ Teach Me ♥

♥ Guide Me ♥

Future Generations

Highlight

My Prayer"s

PSALM 20:4

"Grant thee according
to thine own heart,
and fulfil all thy
counsel".

27

 # Reflect

When you think of fear and doubt, which Bible character pops into your mind? How did they overcome (if at all)? What can you

learn from them

Thank You Lord

Week of: _____

🖤 Teach Me 🖤

🖤 Guide Me 🖤

Future Generations

Highlight

My Prayer"s

LAMENTATIONS 3:22-23

"It is of the Lord's mercies that we are not consumed, because his compassions fail not. They are new every morning: great is thy faithfulness"

31

 # Reflect

> **Job 8:7**
>
> "Your beginnings will seem humble, so prosperous will your future be"

_____
_____
_____
_____
_____
_____
_____
_____
_____
_____
_____
_____
_____
_____
_____
_____
_____
_____
_____

Thank You Lord

 Teach Me

Guide Me

Future Generations

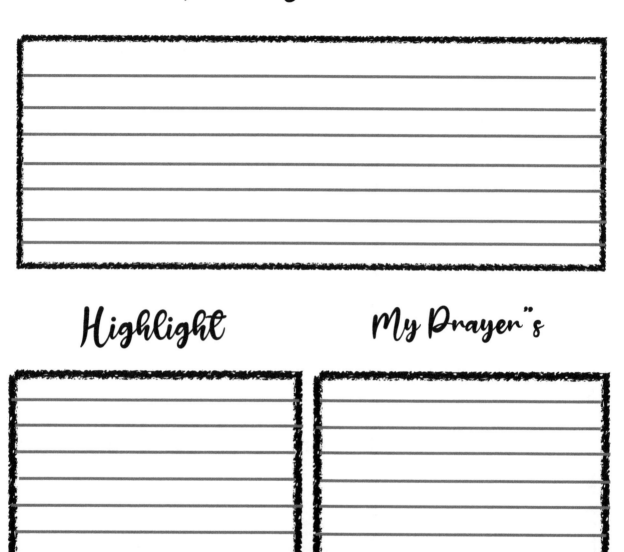

Highlight

My Prayer"s

EPHESIANS 4:32

"be ye kind one to
another, tenderhearted,
forgiving one another,
even as God for Christ's
sake hath forgiven you".

35

 # *Reflect*

Think of one person in your class who needs some comfort and friendship. Describe that:

person and think of one nice thing you could do for him before the school year ends

_____
_____
_____
_____
_____
_____
_____
_____
_____
_____
_____
_____
_____
_____
_____
_____
_____
_____
_____

Thank You Lord

❤ Teach Me ❤

❤ Guide Me ❤

Future Generations

Highlight

My Prayer"s

JAMES 5:16

"Confess your faults one to another, and pray one for another, that ye may be healed. The effectual fervent prayer of a righteous man availeth much"

39

 # Reflect

How can you be a light to others in a dark world?

_____

_____

_____

_____

_____

_____

_____

_____

_____

_____

_____

_____

_____

_____

_____

_____

_____

Thank You Lord

Teach Me

Guide Me

Future Generations

Highlight

My Prayer"s

PROVERBS 28:13

"He that covereth his sins shall not prosper: but whoso confesseth and forsaketh them shall have mercy.".

43

 # Reflect

Describe a time when God used a bad situation
for your good.

_____
_____
_____
_____
_____
_____
_____
_____
_____
_____
_____
_____
_____
_____
_____
_____
_____

Thank You Lord

🖤 Teach Me 🖤

🖤 Guide Me 🖤

Future Generations

Highlight

My Prayer"s

JOSHUA 1:9

"Have not I commanded thee? Be strong and of a good courage; be not afraid, neither be thou dismayed: for the Lord thy God is with thee whithersoever thou goest"

47

 # Reflect

Am I using social media to glorify God or
myself? How can I improve on that?

_____

_____

_____

_____

_____

_____

_____

_____

_____

_____

_____

_____

_____

_____

_____

_____

_____

Thank You Lord

♥ Teach Me ♥

♥ Guide Me ♥

Future Generations

Highlight

My Prayer"s

John 14:27

"Peace I leave with you, my peace I give unto you: not as the world giveth, give I unto you. Let not your heart be troubled, neither let it be afraid".

51

 # Reflect

What does it mean to you to be a person of faith? How important is this to you?

_____
_____
_____
_____
_____
_____
_____
_____
_____
_____
_____
_____
_____
_____
_____
_____
_____
_____
_____

Thank You Lord

Teach Me

Guide Me

Future Generations

Highlight

My Prayer"s

GENESIS 2:3

"God blessed the seventh day, and sanctified it: because that in it he had rested from all his work which God created and made".

55

 # Reflect

When you think of fear and doubt, which Bible character pops into your mind? How did they overcome (if at all)? What can you learn from them?

_____
_____
_____
_____
_____
_____
_____
_____
_____
_____
_____
_____
_____
_____
_____
_____

Thank You Lord

Teach Me

Guide Me

Future Generations

Highlight

My Prayer"s

JEREMIAH 32:17

"Ah Lord God! behold, thou hast made the heaven and the earth by thy great power and stretched out arm, and there is nothing too hard for thee".

59

 # Reflect

Apart from the Bible, what book(s) has impacted your faith greatly? What lessons still resonate with you?

Thank You Lord

🖤 Teach Me 🖤

🖤 Guide Me 🖤

Future Generations

Highlight

My Prayer"s

ROMANS 14:8

"Enerosity For
whether we live, we
live unto the Lord;
and whether we die,
we die unto the Lord:
whether we live
therefore, or die, we
are the Lord's".

63

 # Reflect

How can you curate more faith memories, that is, keep track of all the positive things that happen as a result of your faith in God? Why would this be important?

_____

_____

_____

_____

_____

_____

_____

_____

_____

_____

_____

_____

_____

_____

_____

_____

_____

Thank You Lord

Week of:

Teach Me

Guide Me

Future Generations

Highlight

My Prayer"s

LUKE 23:46

"when Jesus had cried with
a loud voice, he said,
Father, into thy hands I
commend my spirit: and
having said thus, he gave
up the ghost".

67

 # Reflect

How can you keep going in faith
when you are worn out?

Thank You Lord

Week of:

❤ Teach Me ❤

❤ Guide Me ❤

Future Generations

Highlight

My Prayer"s

DEUTERONOMY 31:8

"the Lord, he it is that doth go before thee; he will be with thee, he will not fail thee, neither forsake thee: fear not, neither be dismayed"

71

 # Reflect

What are your thoughts about doubt and faith?
Do you think God frowns at doubt? Do you think
doubt and faith are opposites? What Scriptures
can you draw on to support your thoughts?

Thank You Lord

Teach Me

Guide Me

Future Generations

Highlight

My Prayer"s

JOHN 16:33

"God is my salvation; I will trust and not be afraid. The LORD, the LORD himself, is my strength and my defense; he has become

75

 # Reflect

What thing in nature can you use to prompt your faith? Why have you chosen this symbol?

_____
_____
_____
_____
_____
_____
_____
_____
_____
_____
_____
_____
_____
_____
_____
_____
_____

Thank You Lord

Teach Me

Guide Me

Future Generations

Highlight

My Prayer"s

ROMANS 15:13

" Now the God of hope fill you with all joy and peace in believing, that ye may abound in hope, through the power of the Holy Ghost".

 # Reflect

When you think of faith, what non-Bible quote comes to mind? Write it out. Why does it hold

Thank You Lord

❤ Teach Me ❤

❤ Guide Me ❤

Future Generations

Highlight

My Prayer"s

JOHN 11:40

"Jesus saith unto her,
Said I not unto thee,
that, if thou wouldest
believe, thou shouldest
see the glory of God?"

83

 # Reflect

> What is a belief you have about faith that would surprise someone? What Bible verse did you find that made you develop this belief?

Thank You Lord

Week of:

♥ Teach Me ♥

♥ Guide Me ♥

Future Generations

Highlight

My Prayer"s

PROVERBS 17:9

"He that covereth a transgression seeketh love; but he that repeateth a matter separateth very friends"

87

 # Reflect

> What is the connection between faith and purpose?

Thank You Lord

♥ Teach Me ♥

♥ Guide Me ♥

Future Generations

Highlight

My Prayer"s

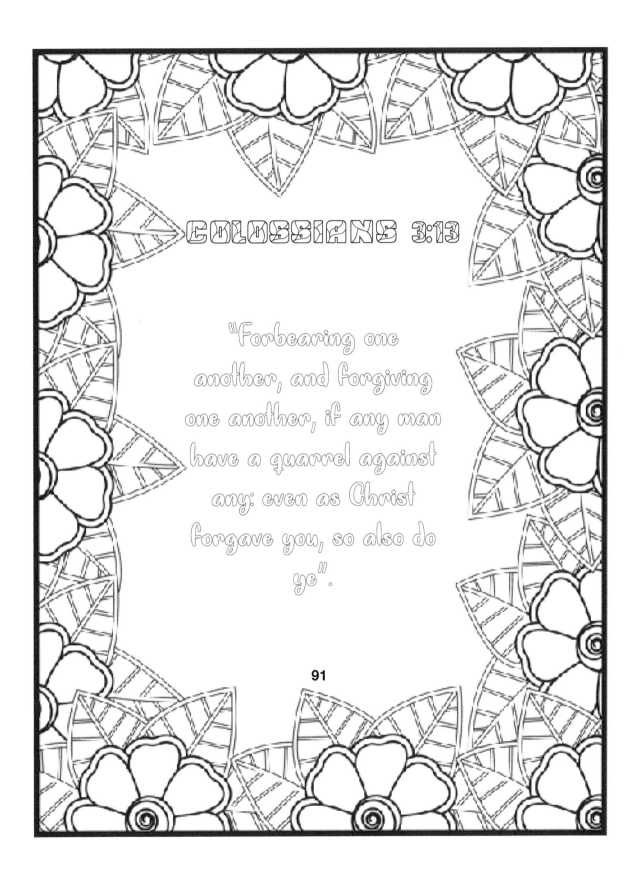

COLOSSIANS 3:13

"Forbearing one another, and forgiving one another, if any man have a quarrel against any: even as Christ forgave you, so also do ye".

91

 # Reflect

What is the most powerful faith story you have ever heard? Why does it resonate with you so much?

_____

_____

_____

_____

_____

_____

_____

_____

_____

_____

_____

_____

_____

_____

_____

_____

_____

_____

Thank You Lord

Teach Me

Guide Me

Future Generations

Highlight

My Prayer"s

ISAIAH 41:10

"Fear thou not; for I am with thee:
be not dismayed; for I am thy God:
I will strengthen thee; yea, I will
help
thee; yea, I will uphold thee with
the right hand of my
righteousness".

95

 # Reflect

How have you leaned on your own
understanding in the past? How did it
affect your faith?

_____
_____
_____
_____
_____
_____
_____
_____
_____
_____
_____
_____
_____
_____
_____
_____
_____
_____
_____
_____

Thank You Lord

♥ Teach Me ♥

_____

_____

_____

_____

_____

♥ Guide Me ♥

_____

_____

_____

_____

Future Generations

Highlight

My Prayer"s

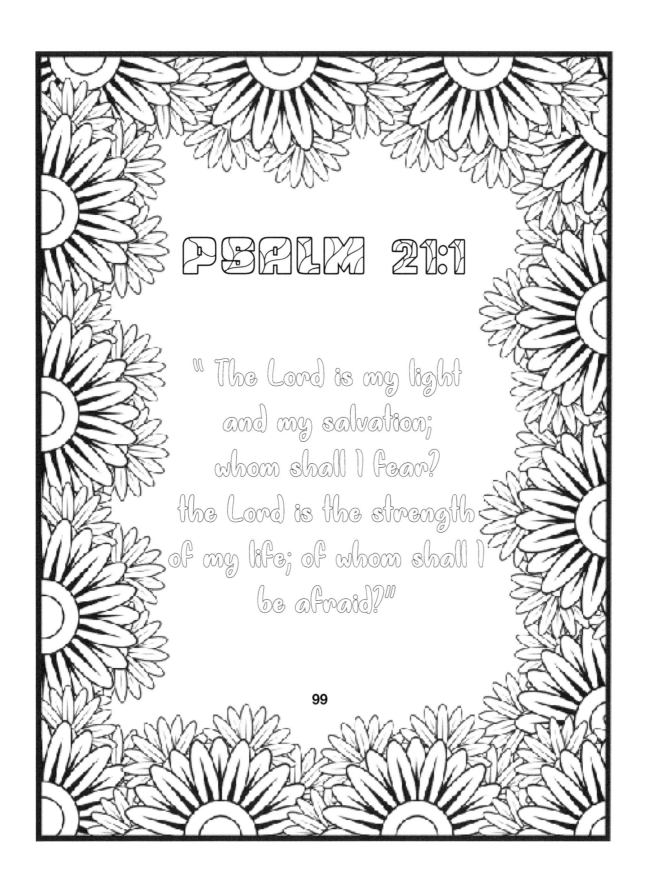

PSALM 21:1

" The Lord is my light
and my salvation;
whom shall I fear?
the Lord is the strength
of my life; of whom shall I
be afraid?"

99

 # Reflect

What friendships are helping your faith?
What can you do to enhance these
friendships?

_____

_____

_____

_____

_____

_____

_____

_____

_____

_____

_____

_____

_____

_____

Thank You Lord

Week of:

Teach Me

Guide Me

Future Generations

Highlight

My Prayer"s

1 JOHN 4:7

"Beloved, let us love one another: for love is of God; and every one that loveth is born of God, and knoweth God".

103

 # Reflect

What friendships are harming your faith? What can you do to set up boundaries or slowly let go of these friendships?

_____
_____
_____
_____
_____
_____
_____
_____
_____
_____
_____
_____
_____
_____
_____
_____
_____
_____

Thank You Lord

Teach Me

Guide Me

Future Generations

Highlight

My Prayer's

1 JOHN 4:21

"And this commandment have we from him, That he who loveth God love his brother also".

107

 # Reflect

To me, this portion of Scripture means…. I can apply it to my life by…..

Thank You Lord

Week of: _____

🖤 Teach Me 🖤

_____
_____
_____
_____
_____
_____
_____

🖤 Guide Me 🖤

_____
_____
_____
_____
_____
_____
_____

Future Generations

Highlight

My Prayer"s

2 CORINTHIANS 9:7

"Every man according as he purposeth in his heart, so let him give; not grudgingly, or of necessity: for God loveth a cheerful giver".

111

 # Reflect

What one thing can I do today to be more like
Jesus based on these Bible verses?

_____

_____

_____

_____

_____

_____

_____

_____

_____

_____

_____

_____

_____

_____

_____

_____

_____

_____

_____

_____

_____

_____

Thank You Lord

♥ Teach Me ♥

♥ Guide Me ♥

Future Generations

Highlight

My Prayer"s

JAMES 1:5

"If any of you lack wisdom, let him ask of God, that giveth to all men liberally, and upbraideth not; and it shall be given him".

 # Reflect

Consider what has happened this past month that you wouldn't have been able to do without God's help. How do you know you couldn't have done it without him?

Thank You Lord

♥ Teach Me ♥

♥ Guide Me ♥

Future Generations

Highlight

My Prayer"s

JEREMIAH 29:10

"I HAVE FOR YOU"
DECLARES THE LORD
"PLANS TO PROSPER
YOU AND NOT TO HARM
YOU. PLANS TO GIVE
YOU HOPE AND A
FUTURE".

119

# Reflect

Faith without works is dead. What does this mean to you?

_____
_____
_____
_____
_____
_____
_____
_____
_____
_____
_____
_____
_____
_____
_____
_____
_____
_____
_____

Thank You Lord

Teach Me

Guide Me

Future Generations

Highlight

My Prayer"s

PSALM 121:7-8

"The Lord shall preserve thee from all evil he shall preserve thy soul. The Lord shall preserve thy going out and thy coming in from this time forth, and even for evermore"

123

 # Reflect

If the Bible were to be rewritten with you as a
character in it, what would you want to be

_____
_____
_____
_____
_____
_____
_____
_____
_____
_____
_____
_____
_____
_____
_____
_____
_____
_____
_____

Week of:

Thank You Lord

Teach Me

Guide Me

Future Generations

Highlight

My Prayer's

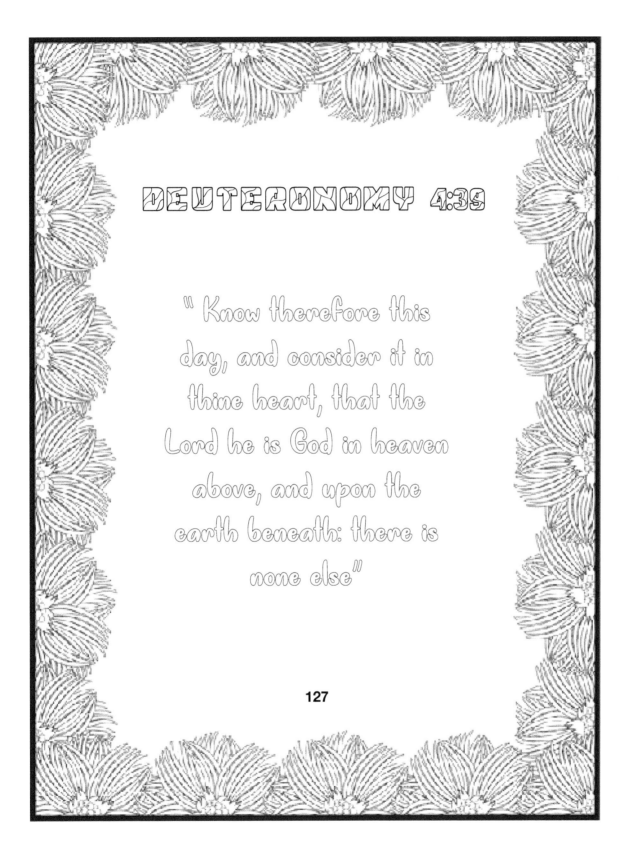

DEUTERONOMY 4:39

" Know therefore this day, and consider it in thine heart, that the Lord he is God in heaven above, and upon the earth beneath: there is none else"

 # Reflect

Which book in the Bible do you go when you're struggling in faith? Why

_____

_____

_____

_____

_____

_____

_____

_____

_____

_____

_____

_____

_____

_____

_____

_____

_____

_____

Thank You Lord

Teach Me

Guide Me

Future Generations

Highlight

My Prayer"s

JOHN 17:15

"I pray not that thou shouldest take them out of the world, but that thou shouldest keep them from the evil".

131

 # Reflect

What's the greatest distraction to your faith right now? What definitive steps can you take to get rid of that distraction?

_____
_____
_____
_____
_____
_____
_____
_____
_____
_____
_____
_____
_____
_____
_____
_____
_____
_____
_____

Thank You Lord

Teach Me

_____
_____
_____
_____
_____
_____
_____
_____

Guide Me

_____
_____
_____
_____
_____
_____

Future Generations

Highlight

My Prayer"s

1 THESSALONIANS 5:16-18

"Rejoice evermore. Pray without ceasing. In every thing give thanks: for this is the will of God in Christ Jesus concerning you".

135

 # Reflect

How does the daily ebb and flow of your emotions affect your faith? How can you improve in this area?

_____
_____
_____
_____
_____
_____
_____
_____
_____
_____
_____
_____
_____
_____
_____
_____
_____
_____
_____
_____
_____
_____

Thank You Lord

🖤 Teach Me 🖤

🖤 Guide Me 🖤

Future Generations

Highlight

My Prayer"s

PSALM 15:11

"Rejoice evermore. Pray without ceasing. In every thing give thanks: for this is the will of God in Christ Jesus concerning you"

139

 # Reflect

> What's the one fear you have that's preventing you from living by faith? What Bible truth can you use to conquer that fear?

Thank You Lord

Week of:

🖤 Teach Me 🖤

🖤 Guide Me 🖤

Future Generations

Highlight

My Prayer"s

ROMANS 6:15

"What then? shall we sin, because we are not under the law, but under grace? God forbid"

 # Reflect

What would your life look like if you stopped
walking in fear and lived by faith?

_____
_____
_____
_____
_____
_____
_____
_____
_____
_____
_____
_____
_____
_____
_____
_____
_____
_____
_____
_____
_____

Thank You Lord

♥ Teach Me ♥

♥ Guide Me ♥

Future Generations

Highlight

My Prayer"s

1 CORINTHIANS 10:23

"All things are lawful for me, but all things are not expedient: all things are lawful for me, but all things edify not".

147

 # Reflect

Is mental health (anxiety, depression, sadness)
an issue for your faith journey?

_____
_____
_____
_____
_____
_____
_____
_____
_____
_____
_____
_____
_____
_____
_____
_____
_____
_____
_____

Thank You Lord

Teach Me

Guide Me

Future Generations

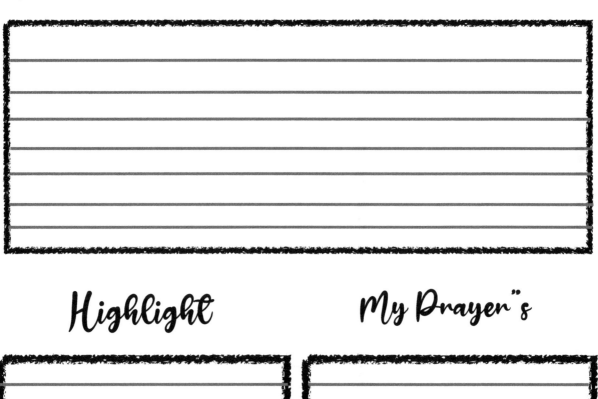

Highlight

My Prayer"s

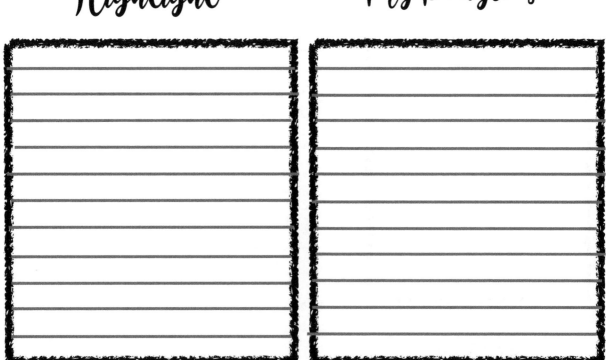

150

HEBREWS 4:16

"Let us therefore come boldly unto the throne of grace, that we may obtain mercy, and find grace to help in time of need.".

151

 # Reflect

Are you getting enough rest? How's your sleep impacting your devotional life and by extension your faith? What small changes could offset improvements in this area.

_____
_____
_____
_____
_____
_____
_____
_____
_____
_____
_____
_____
_____
_____
_____
_____
_____
_____

Thank You Lord

Teach Me

Guide Me

Future Generations

Highlight

My Prayer"s

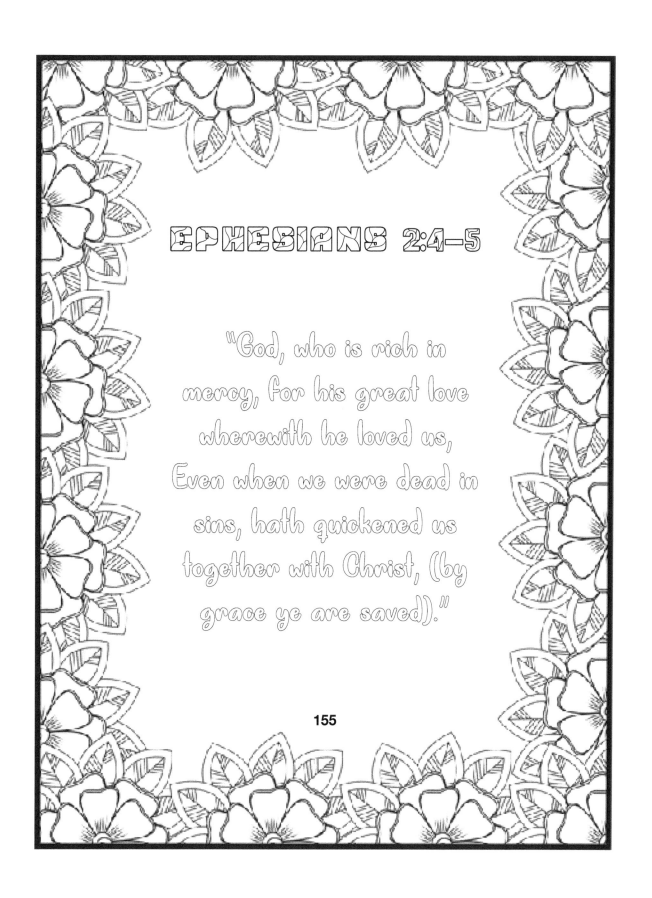

EPHESIANS 2:4-5

"God, who is rich in mercy, for his great love wherewith he loved us, Even when we were dead in sins, hath quickened us together with Christ, ((by grace ye are saved))."

 # Reflect

How has your faith grown over the years? Can you identify specific events that caused your faith to grow? How has your faith changed over the years? And how have you changed as a result of this?

Thank You Lord

Teach Me

Guide Me

Future Generations

Highlight

My Prayer"s

MARK 12:31

"The second is like, namely this, Thou shalt love thy neighbor as thyself. There is none other commandment greater than these".

159

 # Reflect

Think of one person you could help with their faith. What specific thing can you do for or with them?

_____
_____
_____
_____
_____
_____
_____
_____
_____
_____
_____
_____
_____
_____
_____
_____
_____
_____
_____
_____

Thank You Lord

Week of:

Teach Me

Guide Me

Future Generations

Highlight

My Prayer"s

1 PETER 3:8

"Finally, be ye all of one mind, having compassion one of another, love as brethren, be pitiful, be courteous".

 # Reflect

When was the last time you encouraged someone in their faith? How did it go? How did it impact you?

_____
_____
_____
_____
_____
_____
_____
_____
_____
_____
_____
_____
_____
_____
_____
_____
_____
_____
_____

Thank You Lord

Week of:

♥ Teach Me ♥

_____
_____
_____
_____
_____
_____
_____
_____
_____

♥ Guide Me ♥

_____
_____
_____
_____
_____
_____
_____

Future Generations

Highlight

My Prayer"s

PROVERBS 6:20

" My son, keep thy father's commandment, and forsake not the law of thy mother".

167

 # Reflect

How does your relationship with your parents help or hinder your faith?

Thank You Lord

♥ Teach Me ♥

♥ Guide Me ♥

Future Generations

Highlight

My Prayer"s

PROVERBS 10:17

" He is in the way of
life that keepeth
instruction:
but he that refuseth
reproof erreth".

171

Reflect

Have you ever heard God's voice and was disobedient? What were the consequences? How was your faith strengthened or weakened

Thank You Lord

Teach Me

Guide Me

Future Generations

Highlight

My Prayer"s

PROVERBS 14:29

"He that is slow to wrath is of great understanding:but he that is hasty of spirit exalteth folly".

175

 # Reflect

What are your thoughts about doubt and faith?
Do you think God frowns at doubt? Do you think
doubt and faith are opposites? What Scriptures
can you draw on to support your thoughts?

_____
_____
_____
_____
_____
_____
_____
_____
_____
_____
_____
_____
_____
_____
_____
_____
_____
_____

Thank You Lord

Teach Me

Guide Me

Future Generations

Highlight

My Prayer"s

ROMANS 15:5

"Now the God of patience and consolation grant you to be likeminded one toward another according to Christ Jesus"

179

 # Reflect

Write out the song "No Longer Slaves" by Jonathan David and Melissa Helser. What Bible verse(s) is this song built on? Meditate on the song and the Bible verses.

_____
_____
_____
_____
_____
_____
_____
_____
_____
_____
_____
_____
_____
_____
_____
_____
_____
_____
_____
_____
_____

Thank You Lord

Week of:

Teach Me

Guide Me

Future Generations

Highlight

My Prayer"s

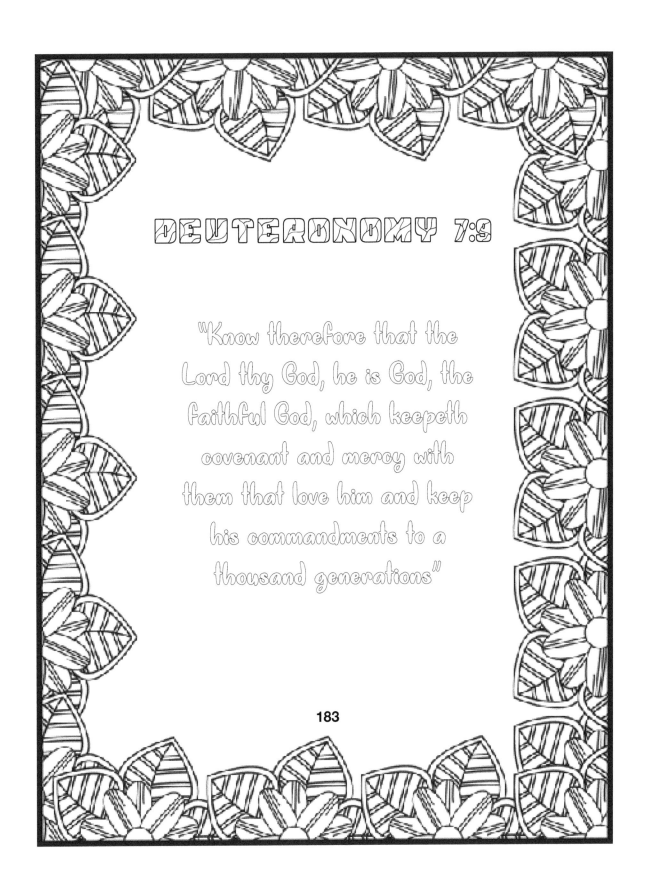

DEUTERONOMY 7:9

"Know therefore that the Lord thy God, he is God, the faithful God, which keepeth covenant and mercy with them that love him and keep his commandments to a thousand generations"

183

 # Reflect

> What thing in nature can you use to prompt your faith? Why have you chosen this symbol?

_____

_____

_____

_____

_____

_____

_____

_____

_____

_____

_____

_____

_____

_____

_____

_____

_____

_____

Thank You Lord

Week of:

♥ Teach Me ♥

♥ Guide Me ♥

Future Generations

Highlight

My Prayer"s

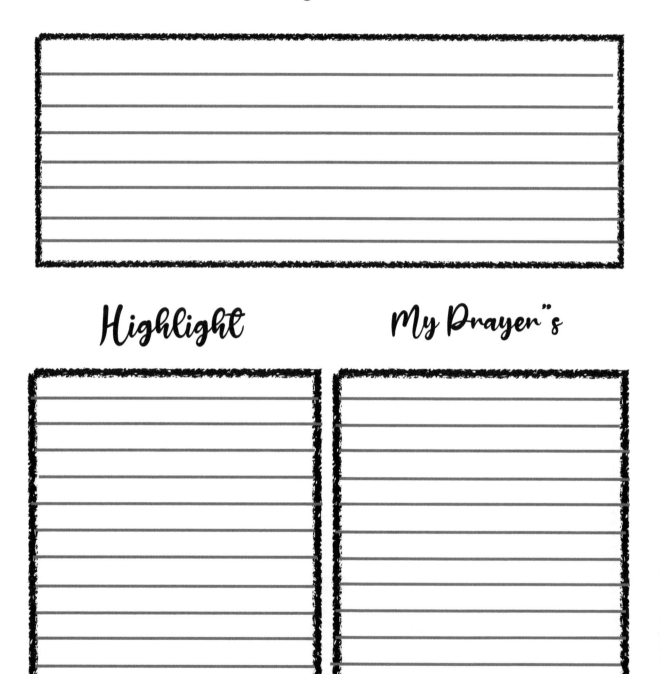

HEBREWS 10:23

"Let us hold fast the profession of our faith without wavering; (for he is faithful that promised;)"

187

 # Reflect

Write about a time you exercised bold faith
that made you very proud of yourself.

_____
_____
_____
_____
_____
_____
_____
_____
_____
_____
_____
_____
_____
_____
_____
_____
_____
_____

Thank You Lord

Teach Me

Guide Me

Future Generations

Highlight

My Prayer"s

PROVERBS 25:28

"He that hath no rule over his own spiritis like a city that is broken down, and without walls".

191

 # Reflect

What is the connection between faith and purpose?

_____
_____
_____
_____
_____
_____
_____
_____
_____
_____
_____
_____
_____
_____
_____
_____
_____
_____
_____
_____

Thank You Lord

Week of:

❤ Teach Me ❤

❤ Guide Me ❤

Future Generations

Highlight

My Prayer"s

2 TIMOTHY 1:7

"For God hath not given us the spirit of fear; but of power, and of love, and of a sound mind".

 # Reflect

Have you noticed that you struggle in faith during certain seasons or when it comes to certain aspects of your life? What are those times? What can you do to be more aware? What can you to exercise stable faith during those times?

_____
_____
_____
_____
_____
_____
_____
_____
_____
_____
_____
_____
_____
_____
_____
_____
_____
_____
_____
_____
_____

Thank You Lord

🖤 Teach Me 🖤

🖤 Guide Me 🖤

Future Generations

Highlight

My Prayer"s

JAMES 1:12

"Blessed is the man that endureth temptation: for when he is tried, he shall receive the crown of life, which the Lord hath promised to them that love him".

199

 # Reflect

Do you think faith and logic have anything to do with each other? What Bible verses can you use to support your thoughts?

_____
_____
_____
_____
_____
_____
_____
_____
_____
_____
_____
_____
_____
_____
_____
_____
_____
_____
_____

Thank You Lord

Teach Me

Guide Me

Future Generations

Highlight

My Prayer"s

MATHEW 26:41

"Watch and pray, that ye enter not into temptation: the spirit indeed is willing, but the flesh is weak".

203

 # Reflect

Write about someone whose faith you admire and why.

Thank You Lord

Teach Me

Guide Me

Future Generations

Highlight

My Prayer"s

PROVERBS 3:5-6

"Trust in the Lord with all thine heart; and lean not unto thine own understanding. In all thy ways acknowledge him, and he shall direct thy paths"

 # Reflect

What are misconceptions you've held about faith?
When did you realize it? Where are you now in
your thoughts about those misconceptions?

_____
_____
_____
_____
_____
_____
_____
_____
_____
_____
_____
_____
_____
_____
_____
_____
_____
_____
_____

Thank You Lord

Week of:

♥ Teach Me ♥

♥ Guide Me ♥

Future Generations

Highlight

My Prayer"s

PROVERBS 16:3

"Commit thy works unto the Lord, and thy thoughts shall be established".

211

 # Reflect

Scripture says faith is a gift. How are you sure that you have accepted that gift?

Thank You Lord

 **Teach Me**

 **Guide Me**

Future Generations

Highlight

My Prayer"s

JEREMIAH 33:3

"Call unto me, and I will answer thee, and show thee great and mighty things, which thou knowest not".

215

 # Reflect

What does trusting God completely look like?

Sound like?

_____

_____
_____
_____
_____
_____
_____
_____
_____
_____
_____
_____
_____
_____
_____
_____
_____
_____
_____
_____
_____

Thank You Lord

Teach Me

Guide Me

Future Generations

Highlight

My Prayer"s

PROVERBS 4:7

"Wisdom is the principal thing; therefore get wisdom: and with all thy getting get understanding".

219

 # Reflect

Really think about this: do you see God as an ATM or someone to have a daily abiding relationship with? Why do you trust him? What's the basis of your relationship with God?

_____
_____
_____
_____
_____
_____
_____
_____
_____
_____
_____
_____
_____
_____
_____
_____
_____
_____
_____
_____

Thank You Lord

Week of: _____

🌳 Teach Me 🌳

🌳 Guide Me 🌳

Future Generations

Highlight

My Prayer"s

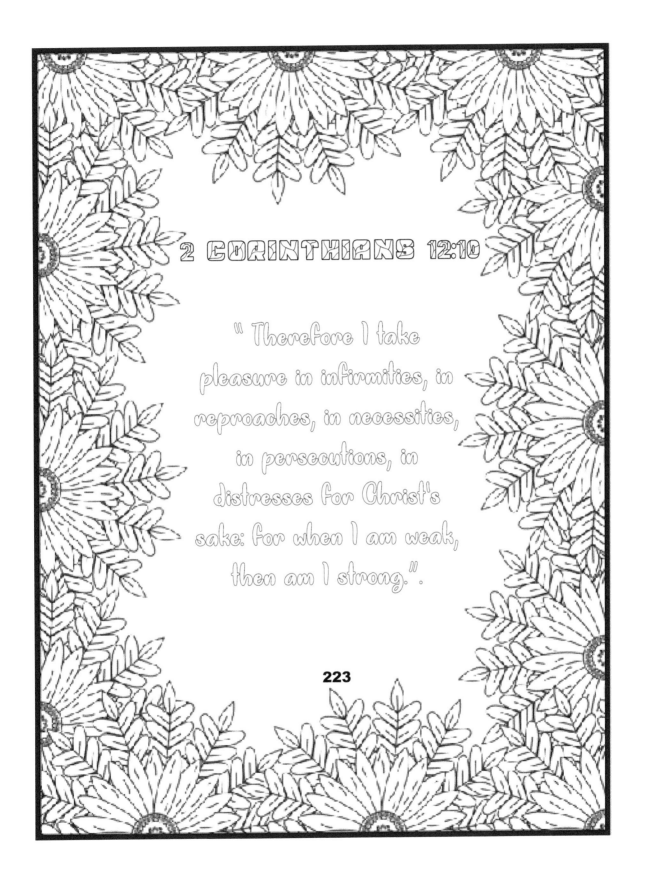

2 CORINTHIANS 12:10

" Therefore I take pleasure in infirmities, in reproaches, in necessities, in persecutions, in distresses for Christ's sake: for when I am weak, then am I strong.".

223

 # Reflect

Read some of your old reflections. How has God shown up for you in the past that can make you feel more confident that he will show up for you now?

_____
_____
_____
_____
_____
_____
_____
_____
_____
_____
_____
_____
_____
_____
_____
_____
_____
_____
_____
_____
_____

Thank You Lord

Week of:

♥ Teach Me ♥

♥ Guide Me ♥

Future Generations

Highlight

My Prayer's

My Prayer"s

My Prayer"s

My Prayer"s

My Prayer"s

My Prayer"s

My Prayer"s

My Prayer"s

My Prayer"s

CPSIA information can be obtained
at www.ICGtesting.com
Printed in the USA
LVHW110819240222
711902LV00004B/48

9 780578 372822